THE YOUTUBE FILMING HANDBOOK:

Essential Tips and Tricks for Filming Professional Quality Videos.

Benjamin Williams

THE YOUTUBE
FILMING HANDBOOK

ESSENTIAL TIPS AND TRICKS FOR FILMING PROFESSIONAL QUALITY VIDEOS.

BENJAMIN WILLIAMS

CONTENTS

BENJAMIN WILLIAMS

The YouTube Filming Handbook: Essential Tips and Tricks for Filming Professional Quality Videos.

INTRODUCTION

Welcome to another YouTube guide from our YouTube success in 2023 series. In this guide, we will be covering the essential elements of filming for the successful production of YouTube videos. From choosing the right location and setting up the perfect shot, to mastering the art of post-production, we will provide you with the tools and techniques you need to create high-quality content that engages and entertains your audience.

Filming for YouTube requires taking into account a few unique aspects that differ from traditional film and television production. One key difference is the platform's focus on digital content, which means that videos need to be optimized for online viewing. This includes considering factors such as resolution, frame rate, and file size, as well as ensuring that the video is compatible with various devices and internet speeds.

Unlike traditional media, YouTube's platform emphasizes audience engagement and interaction. Successful YouTubers often incorporate elements such as call-to-actions, interactive challenges, and behind-the-scenes glimpses in their videos to encourage viewer participation and build a sense of community.

Additionally, YouTube content creators often have to juggle multiple roles and responsibilities, from filming and editing to marketing and branding. This means that they need to be proficient in a wide range of skills and be able to adapt to the constantly evolving nature of the platform.

Not only this, but YouTube is known for its diverse and ever-expanding content offerings, which means that filmmakers need to be mindful of the specific conventions and expectations of their chosen niche or genre. Whether it's unboxing videos, gaming streams, or educational content, understanding the unique characteristics of the YouTube ecosystem is crucial for success.

All these things need to be taken into account when creating your shooting schedule, how you set up your shots and your subsequent editing phase (which we will discuss in our next book).

This guide will look over the foundational levels of planning and executing your shoots. For example, choosing the right location is crucial for creating high-quality videos, as it can greatly affect the overall look and feel of your content. This planning will help showcase the purpose of your video and the type of atmosphere you want to create, as well as lighting and background factors.

Once we have planned, our next step is organizing the both shot composition and proper lighting. Both understanding and utilizing proper lighting is an essential element of any successful video, and can make a huge difference in the quality of your footage. Whether you are using natural light or artificial light sources, it's important to consider the direction and intensity of the light, as well as any shadows that may be present.

This mix of technical understanding and understanding the demands of YouTube and the dreaded algorithm is vital to success in 2023.

Let's jump in.

CHAPTER 1: FILMING

Whether you are a beginner or an experienced filmmaker, there are always new techniques and tips to learn when it comes to creating high-quality content for the platform. In the following chapters, we will cover topics such as planning and preparing for a shoot, choosing the right location and lighting, and setting up your camera and equipment. By the end of this chapter, you will have a solid foundation in the basic principles of YouTube filming and be well on your way to creating professional and engaging videos for your audience.

It is something you may do on a daily basis, and you probably already know these terms and concepts already, but I want us to build our knowledge from the ground up, understanding the basics so we can become masters later.

Our Foundation

Filming: Filming is the process of capturing video footage using a camera, typically with the goal of creating a cohesive, engaging visual narrative. As a film student, it's important to have a strong understanding of the technical aspects of filming in order to create professional-quality videos. Here are some key considerations when filming:

Composition: This refers to the way that elements within the frame are arranged, including the placement of subjects, the use of leading lines, and the overall balance of the image. Good composition can help to create a sense of depth, movement, and visual interest.

Lighting: Proper lighting is crucial for creating high-quality footage, as it can bring out the detail and texture of your subjects and set the mood of your scene. Lighting can be natural or artificial, and it's important to consider the direction, intensity, and color temperature of the light.

Sound: Capturing clear audio is essential for bringing your footage to life and engaging your audience. This includes capturing dialogue, music, and sound effects, as well as considering the overall sound design of your film.

Cinematography: This refers to the technical aspects of filming, including camera movement, lens choice, and shot composition. By understanding the principles of cinematography, you can create dynamic, visually striking shots that enhance the storytelling of your film.

Storytelling: At the heart of any good film is a strong narrative that engages and entertains the audience. This includes having a clear understanding of your goals and target audience, as well as using techniques such as character development, plot structure, and visual storytelling to convey your message.

By understanding the basics of these technical and creative aspects of filming, you can create professional-quality videos that engage and entertain your audience. Whether you are just starting out in film school or are an experienced filmmaker, these principles will help you create compelling, visually striking content that stands out from the competition.

Planning Ahead

Planning ahead was something I had no interest in when I first began my journey but planning ahead is crucial when it comes to creating a successful YouTube video. Before you start filming, it's important to take some time to think about the purpose, audience, and message of your video, as well as the structure and flow. This will help to ensure that you are clear and focused about your goals and objectives, and it will also help you to create a more impactful and effective video.

First and foremost, it's important to consider the purpose of your video. What are you trying to achieve with your content? Are you trying to inform, educate, entertain, or inspire your viewers? Having a clear idea of your purpose will help you to create a more focused and effective video.

Next, it's important to consider your audience. Who are you trying to reach with your video? Consider the demographics, interests, and preferences of the people you are trying to engage.

This will help you to create a video that resonates with your audience and meets their needs.

It's also important to have a clear and concise message that you want to convey through your video. This message should be central to your content and should drive the structure and flow of your video. By having a clear and focused message, you can create a more impactful and effective video.

Finally, it's important to consider the structure and flow of your video. Will you use a linear or non-linear structure? Will you use narration, music, or other audio elements to enhance your content? Having a clear idea of the structure and flow of your video will help you to create a more cohesive and engaging video.

CHAPTER 2: TECHNICAL TIPS

Utilizing a Tripod

Even if you are simply using your smartphone to film, using a tripod is a key element of filming a YouTube video, as it helps to keep the camera steady and eliminate camera shake. This is especially important if you're shooting with a long lens or in low light conditions, as these factors can make it more difficult to keep the camera steady.

Stability is one of the main benefits of using a tripod when filming a YouTube video. A tripod helps to keep your camera steady and reduces the risk of camera shake, which can be particularly noticeable when shooting with a long lens or in low light conditions. This can create a smoother and more professional-looking video, as it will be easier for your viewers to focus on the content of your video rather than being distracted by shaky footage.

Using a tripod can also help to ensure that your shots are consistent and have a uniform look. For example, if you are filming a series of shots with different camera angles, a tripod can help to keep the camera at a consistent height and prevent shots from looking too jerky or disorienting.

In addition to stability and consistency, using a tripod can also be useful for helping you to compose your shots more accurately and precisely. By using a tripod, you can adjust the height and angle of your camera more easily and take your time to get the perfect shot.

Resolution Rate

Another thing I overlooked which ended up costing me a lot of time in the production stage was resolution rate. It's important to set the right resolution and frame rate when filming a YouTube video, as this can have a big impact on the quality and visual appeal of your final product.

Resolution refers to the number of pixels in an image, and it is typically measured in width x height (e.g. 1920 x 1080 pixels). The higher the resolution, the more detailed and clear the image will be. 1080p (1920 x 1080 pixels) is a common resolution for YouTube videos, as it provides a good balance between detail and file size.

However, if you are shooting in 4K (3840 x 2160 pixels) or higher, you may want to consider using a higher resolution to capture more detail and provide a better viewing experience for your viewers.

Frame rate refers to the number of frames per second (fps) in a video, and it is typically measured in fps. The higher the frame rate, the smoother and more fluid the video will appear. Most YouTube videos are shot at 30 fps, which is a good frame rate for most videos. However, if you are shooting action or sports, you may want to consider using a higher frame rate to capture more detail and provide a more realistic viewing experience. For example, some cameras and software can support frame rates of 60 fps or higher, which can be useful for capturing fast-moving action.

Remember, setting the right resolution and frame rate from the beginning for your YouTube video, you can help to ensure that your final product looks its best and is enjoyable for your viewers and can save you hours in the long run.

Automatic or Manual Exposure?

Using manual exposure settings when filming a YouTube video can give you more control over the look and feel of your final product. *Remember, the final product is king.*

Exposure refers to the amount of light that is captured by the camera, and it is determined by three main factors: aperture, shutter speed, and ISO.

Aperture is the size of the camera's lens opening, and it controls the amount of light that enters the camera. A larger aperture (i.e. a smaller f-number) allows more light to enter the camera, which can be useful for low light conditions. A smaller aperture (i.e. a larger f-number) allows less light to enter the camera, which can be useful for bright conditions or for creating a shallow depth of field (i.e. a blurry background).

Shutter speed refers to the length of time that the camera's shutter is open, and it controls the amount of light that is captured by the camera. A slower shutter speed allows more light to enter the camera, which can be useful for low light conditions. A faster shutter speed allows less light to enter the camera, which can be useful for freezing fast-moving action or reducing motion blur.

ISO is the camera's sensitivity to light, and it controls the amount of light that is captured by the camera. A higher ISO allows the camera to be more sensitive to light, which can be useful for low light conditions. However, a higher ISO can also result in more noise (i.e. grain) in the image, which can reduce image quality.

If you are using a camera which isn't a smartphone, utilizing these three manual exposure settings (aperture, shutter speed, and ISO), you can fine-tune the exposure of your YouTube videos and create the desired look and feel for your content.

Utilizing Different Lenses

Even if you are not planning on using a camera with lenses,

it is important to understand the different effects that different lens focal lengths can create. A lens focal length is the distance between the lens and the image sensor of a camera, and it determines the field of view and the magnification of the image.

A wide-angle lens has a short focal length, typically between 10mm and 35mm, and gives a wide field of view. This can be useful for creating sweeping landscapes or for capturing a large area in a single shot. Wide-angle lenses are also good for exaggerating the size of objects in the foreground, which can create a sense of depth and scale in your shots.

A telephoto lens, on the other hand, has a longer focal length, typically between 70mm and 200mm, and gives a narrow field of view. This can be useful for compressing the distance between objects, which can make them appear closer together in the frame. Telephoto lenses are also good for creating a more intimate shot, as they allow you to zoom in on a subject and fill the frame with it.

You can find extensions for your phone which will mimic these lenses and if you are using an actual camera, understanding these lenses allows you the ability to add them to your filming schedule and ultimately produce a more professional looking product

White Balance

If you've ever noticed that the colors in your videos look a bit off, it could be due to incorrect white balance. White balance is the process of adjusting the colors in your footage so that whites appear white under different lighting conditions. Proper white balance is crucial for creating natural-looking colors and ensuring that your footage looks professional.

On your camera - White balance is a camera setting that helps to ensure that the colors in your video look natural and accurate. It adjusts the camera's color temperature to match the lighting conditions of your scene, so that whites and other colors appear as they would in real life.

When the white balance is not set correctly, the colors in your video may appear too warm (yellow/orange) or too cool (blue). This can be particularly noticeable when shooting under different types of lighting, such as incandescent, fluorescent, or natural light.

There are several ways to set white balance in a camera. One option is to use the automatic white balance setting, which adjusts the white balance automatically based on the lighting conditions. However, this may not always produce the most accurate results, especially in tricky lighting situations.

Another option is to use a custom white balance setting, which allows you to set the white balance manually by taking a reference photo of a neutral grey or white object in the scene. This helps to ensure that the white balance is accurately set for the specific lighting conditions of the scene.

In general, it's a good idea to set the white balance manually if you have the option, as this gives you more control over the final look of your video. However, it's also important to keep in mind that white balance is a creative tool, and you can use it to intentionally shift the colors in your video to achieve a specific look or mood.

Does the iPhone Account for White Balance When Filming?

I know this won't pertain to everyone, but yes, the iPhone does account for white balance when filming. The iPhone has an automatic white balance feature that adjusts the camera's color temperature to match the lighting conditions of the scene. This helps to ensure that the colors in your video look natural and accurate.

However, it's important to note that the automatic white balance setting may not always produce the most accurate results, especially in tricky lighting situations. If you want more control over the white balance in your videos, you can use the manual white balance setting on your iPhone.

To set the white balance manually on an iPhone, go to the "Camera" app and tap the "WB" (white balance) icon. From there, you can choose from a range of presets (such as "sunny," "cloudy," or "incandescent") or use the "custom" option to set the white balance manually by taking a reference photo of a neutral grey or white object in the scene.

Remember, white balance is a creative tool, and you can use it to intentionally shift the colors in your video to achieve a specific look or mood. Experiment with different white balance settings to find what works best for your particular scene and camera setup.

CHAPTER 3: THE RULE OF THIRDS

4:3 Aspect Ratio with Rule of Thirds

What Is the Rule of Thirds?

Something that I am glad I learned early, was the rule of thirds. The rule of thirds is a widely used technique in photography that helps to frame the main subject of a photo in a way that creates balance and dynamism. It is based on the idea of dividing the frame into a 3x3 grid and placing the main subject at one of the intersections of the grid lines. This can be achieved by using a grid overlay in the viewfinder or LCD screen of a camera, which is a feature that is available on most digital cameras. The goal of using the rule of thirds is to make the photo more visually appealing by avoiding the placement of the main subject in the center of the frame. Instead, the subject is positioned at the top, bottom, left, or right of the grid, which draws the viewer's eye to one of the points of interest and creates a more engaging experience.

How Does it Work?

The rule of thirds works by guiding the placement of the main subject in a way that takes into account how the human eye naturally views an image. When looking at a photo, the eye is drawn to points beyond the center, which are known as the intersecting points on a rule of thirds grid. Studies have shown that people tend to read images from left to right in the same way that they read text, which means that the bottom right portion of an image is more likely to be visually appealing. In contrast, the upper left part of the image is more likely to be overlooked. By using the rule of thirds to position the main subject at one of the intersecting points, a photographer can create a more balanced and dynamic image that captures the viewer's attention.

Why is the Rule of Thirds Important to Follow?

The importance of the rule of thirds lies in its ability to create balance and dynamism in photos. By positioning the main subject at one of the intersections of the grid lines, the photo becomes more balanced because the subject occupies one third of the composition while the remaining two-thirds of the frame is left open. This allows for the use of negative space and helps to draw the viewer's attention to the subject. In contrast, placing the subject in the center of the frame can create a static and uninteresting image. On the other hand, using the rule of thirds adds dynamism because the viewer's eye is drawn to the subject and then travels through the rest of the photo. Additionally, the rule of thirds aligns with the way the human eye naturally views an image, making it a useful tool for creating engaging and visually appealing photos.

Utilizing the Rule in Your Work

To effectively use the rule of thirds in photography, there are several steps that you can follow:

1.   Enable the grid overlay feature in the viewfinder or LCD screen of your camera or mobile device. This will help you to compose your shots on the move.

2.   Experiment with placing the main subject at different intersections of the grid by taking multiple photos with the subject in different positions.

3.   Take a photo of the subject in the center of the frame for comparison.

4.   Review all of the photos that you have taken and choose the ones that you like the best.

5.   Show the photos to a photographer or someone with a good eye for composition and ask for their opinion on which ones are the strongest.

6.   When cropping your photos in editing software, such as Photoshop, Lightroom, or Luminar, use the grid overlay feature to help you crop the photo in a way that follows the rule of thirds.

I have found that by understanding and following these steps, you can learn to effectively use the rule of thirds in your photography and create eye-catching images that are balanced and dynamic.

To use the rule of thirds when filming a YouTube video, try to position the main subject or point of interest along one of the horizontal lines or at one of the intersections of the lines. For example, if you are filming a person, you might position their eyes along the top horizontal line, or if you are filming a landscape, you might position the horizon along the bottom horizontal line.

Remember, with most of these tips, the rule of thirds is not a hard and fast rule, and it is not always necessary or appropriate to use it. However, it can be a useful tool for helping to compose shots that are visually balanced and aesthetically pleasing. By keeping the rule of thirds in mind when filming your YouTube videos, you can create more visually appealing and engaging content for your viewers.

But I want to Screen Record – Not Film

Now this is for those wanting to make Let's Play videos or those creating something like an instructional video for a program and who are not wanting to film themselves.

There are many screen recording software options available for creating "Let's Play" videos on YouTube. Here are a few of the best screen recorders for this purpose:

1.   OBS Studio (*My personal favorite*): OBS Studio is a free, open-source screen recording and streaming software that is widely used by YouTubers and streamers. It has a wide range of features,

including the ability to record from multiple sources, such as your desktop, webcam, and microphone, and to add overlays and text to your recordings.

2.   Bandicam: Bandicam is a paid screen recording software that is popular among YouTubers and streamers. It has a range of features, including the ability to record in high definition, to add webcam and microphone audio to your recordings, and to schedule recordings.

3.   ScreenFlow: ScreenFlow is a paid screen recording and video editing software that is popular among Mac users. It has a range of features, including the ability to record from multiple sources, to add annotations and text to your recordings, and to edit and enhance your recordings with professional-grade video editing tools.

4.   Camtasia: Camtasia is a paid screen recording and video editing software that is popular among YouTubers and educators. It has a range of features, including the ability to record from multiple sources, to add annotations and callouts to your recordings, and to edit and enhance your recordings with professional-grade video editing tools.

Should I follow the basic rules of filming if I am screen recording for a video?

Yes, it is generally a good idea to follow the basic rules of filming when screen recording for a video, even though you are not capturing footage with a traditional camera. These rules can help to ensure that your screen recordings are visually appealing and easy to follow for your viewers.

Because lighting and your recording setup may not be factors, the most important thing to remember when recording is cinematography and framing your shots.

Frame your shots: Pay attention to the composition of your screen recordings, and make sure that your content is properly framed and easy to see. Avoid recording with too much empty space around the edges of the screen, and try to use the "rule of thirds" from our previous section to create visually appealing compositions.

Even without traditional filming, properly framing your shots is an important aspect of creating engaging and professional screen recordings for your YouTube videos.

To frame your shots effectively, try to avoid recording with too much empty space around the edges of the screen. This can make your content feel disconnected or unbalanced, and it can distract your viewers from the main focus of the shot.

Instead, try to fill the frame with your content and leave just enough space around the edges to create visual interest and balance.

CHAPTER 4:
CINEMATOGRAPHY

Cinematography is the art and technique of capturing motion pictures on film or digitally. It encompasses a wide range of technical and creative elements, including camera movement, lens choice, and shot composition. By understanding the principles of cinematography, you can create dynamic, visually striking shots that enhance the storytelling of your film.

One key aspect of cinematography is camera movement, which refers to the way that the camera is positioned and moved during filming. Camera movement can include techniques such as panning, tilting, dollying, and craning, and it can be used to create a sense of motion, depth, and visual interest.

Lens choice is another important aspect of cinematography, as the lens that you use can have a significant impact on the look and feel of your footage. Different lenses have different focal lengths, which can affect the way that your shots are framed and the depth of field that is visible. By choosing the right lens for the job, you can create visually striking shots that draw your audience into the story.

Shot composition is another key element of cinematography, as it refers to the way that elements within the frame are arranged. This includes the placement of subjects, the use of leading lines, and the overall balance of the image. By understanding the principles of shot composition, you can create visually appealing, aesthetically pleasing shots that engage your audience.

Remember, our goal of understanding these basic technical and creative aspects of cinematography, is so that you can create professional-quality videos that engage and entertain your audience. Creating content which is compelling, visually striking content that will help you stand out from the competition. This will give you more views, more subs and help establish yourself a brand, which you can then monetize, something I cover in my other books in the series.

Shot Composition

Shot composition refers to the way that elements within the frame of a video are arranged and the overall visual impact of the shot. Good shot composition can help to engage your viewers and convey your message effectively.

There are a few key factors to consider when it comes to shot composition. The first is the placement of the subject within the frame. The subject of your shot is the main focus of the shot, and where you place it within the frame can have a big impact on the overall impact of the shot. For example, placing the subject off-center can create a more dynamic and visually interesting shot.

Another important factor to consider is the use of negative space.

Negative space is the area around the subject of the shot. Including negative space in your shot can help to create balance and draw the viewer's eye to the subject.

The use of leading lines is another effective technique for creating good shot composition. Leading lines are lines within the frame that draw the viewer's eye towards the subject. These can be actual lines, such as the edge of a table or a road, or they can be implied lines, such as the direction a person is looking or the angle of a camera shot.

The best YouTube stars utilize these techniques effectively to create engaging and visually interesting videos. By taking the time to plan and execute good shot composition, you can create a video that captures the attention of your viewers and effectively conveys your message.

Negative Space

Negative space, also known as white space, is the area around the subject of a shot in a video. It is the opposite of positive space, which is the subject itself. Negative space can be an important element in shot composition, as it helps to create balance and draw the viewer's eye to the subject.

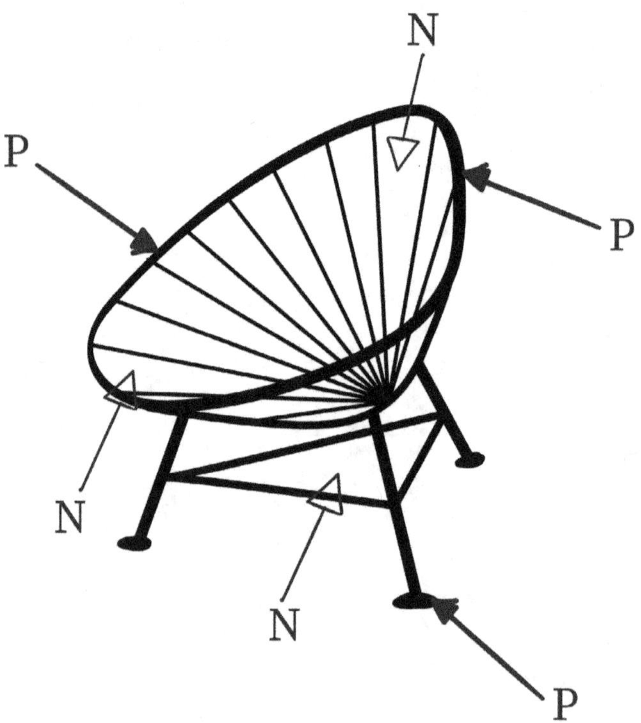

P - Positive Space
N - Negative Space

There are a few key ways to use negative space effectively in filming:

1.   Create balance: Negative space can help to balance the composition of a shot by providing a visual counterpoint to the subject. This can be especially useful if the subject is large or occupies a significant portion of the frame.

2.   Draw the viewer's eye: Negative space can help to draw the viewer's eye to the subject by providing a clear visual path. This can be achieved by positioning the subject towards the center of the frame and leaving more negative space around the edges.

3.   Create a sense of depth: Negative space can also be used to create a sense of depth in a shot. For example, placing the subject in the foreground and leaving more negative space in the background can give the impression that the subject is closer to the viewer.

4.   Provide context: Negative space can also provide context for the subject of a shot. For example, if you are shooting a person, the negative space around them can help to convey the location or setting in which they are located.

Overall, negative space is a powerful tool for creating visually interesting and effective shots in video. By using negative space effectively, you can create shots that are balanced, engaging, and visually appealing.

Is there a specific ratio needed for Negative Space?

There are no specific ratios for the effective use of negative space in filming, as the right balance will depend on the specific needs of your shot. That being said, there are a few general guidelines you can follow to ensure that you are using negative space effectively:

1.   Consider the size and placement of the subject: The size and placement of the subject within the frame will affect the balance of positive and negative space in the shot. For example, a large subject placed towards the center of the frame will leave more negative space around the edges, while a smaller subject placed towards the edge of the frame will leave more negative space in the center.

2.   Use negative space to create balance: Negative space can help to balance the composition of a shot by providing a visual counterpoint to the subject. This can be especially useful if the subject is large or occupies a significant portion of the frame.

3.   Use negative space to draw the viewer's eye: Negative space can also be used to draw the viewer's eye to the subject by providing a clear visual path. This can be achieved by positioning the subject towards the center of the frame and leaving more negative space around the edges.

4.   Experiment with different ratios: The best way to determine the right balance of positive and negative space for your shot is to experiment with different ratios. Try shooting with different amounts of negative space and see what works best for your particular shot.

CHAPTER 5: LIGHTING

Lighting Lighting Lighting!

Good lighting can make or break a video, it can make a difference how professional a video will look which has a huge impact on your final analytics (views, subs, etc) Even small changes to lighting and basic understanding of the fundamentals can be provide a significant difference in the overall quality and impact of your videos. It can help to set the mood and tone of your shots, as well as highlight the subject and create visual interest.

There are a few key factors to consider when it comes to lighting in filming:

1.   Natural light: Natural light can be a great source of lighting for your videos. The key is to pay attention to the direction and intensity of the light and how it affects your shots. For example, shooting with the sun behind your subject can create a silhouette effect, while shooting with the sun in front of your subject can create harsh shadows.

2.   Artificial light: Artificial light can be used to supplement or replace natural light in your shots. There are many different types

of artificial light sources available, including tungsten lights, fluorescent lights, and LED lights, each with their own unique characteristics. The key is to choose the right light source for your particular needs and to experiment with different lighting setups to find what works best.

3.   Color temperature: The color temperature of a light source refers to the hue of the light. Different color temperatures can create different moods and effects in your shots. For example, warm light sources, such as tungsten lights, can create a cozy, warm atmosphere, while cool light sources, such as fluorescent lights, can create a more clinical, neutral atmosphere.

4.   Light intensity: The intensity of a light source refers to how bright or dim it is. Adjusting the intensity of your lights can help to create different moods and effects in your shots. For example, using low-intensity lighting can create a moody, atmospheric shot, while using high-intensity lighting can create a more dramatic, vibrant shot.

Remember, lighting is an essential element of good video production. By understanding the different characteristics of light and how to use it effectively, you can create professional-looking shots that engage your viewers and convey your message effectively.

3-Point Lighting System

A 3-point lighting system is a basic lighting setup that is commonly used in film and television production to create professional-quality lighting for interviews, talking heads, and other types of footage. It involves the use of three separate lights: a key light, a fill light, and a back light.

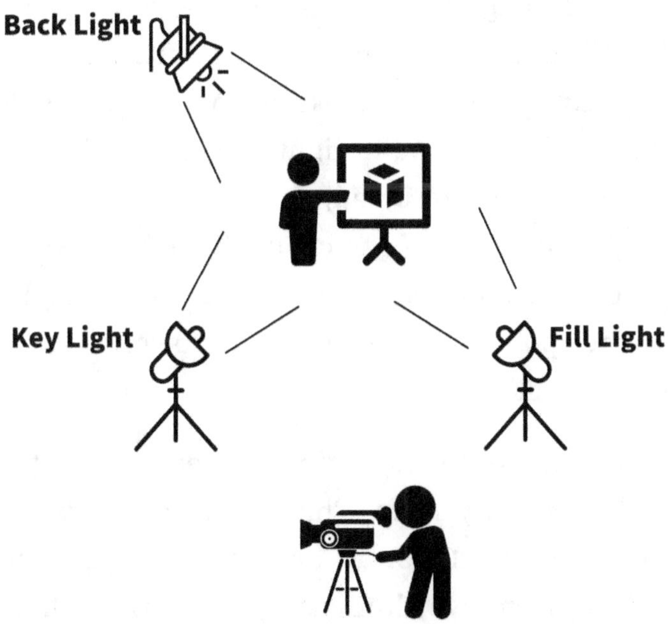

There are several reasons why a three-point lighting system is useful in video production. One of the main benefits is that it helps to make the video or live stream look more professional and polished. By carefully controlling the direction and intensity of the light, a three-point lighting system can reduce shadows and make the subject's face more visible, which is especially important for creating clear and engaging video content.

Additionally, using a three-point lighting system can help to improve the separation between the subject and the background, which is especially useful when using a green screen or virtual background. This makes it easier to replace the background in post-production and creates a more seamless and realistic final result.

Another benefit of using a three-point lighting system is that it adds dimension to the subject. By using a key light, fill light, and back light, the three-point lighting system creates a sense of depth and helps to define the edges of the subject. This can be especially useful for creating more visually interesting and dynamic video content. Additionally, the three-point lighting system allows for flexibility and experimentation. By adjusting the direction and intensity of the lights, it is possible to create different looks and moods, such as a soft and optimistic look or a dramatic and dark look. Overall, the three-point lighting system is a powerful tool for creating professional-quality video content.

In three-point lighting, the relationship between the lights is known as the light intensity ratio. This refers to the relative brightness of each light in relation to one another. A common light intensity ratio for narrative filmmaking and YouTube videos is 2:1, which means that the key light should be twice as bright as the fill light.

However, this ratio may need to be adjusted depending on the specific goals of the video. For example, in a commercial or corporate video, a ratio of 1.5:1 may be more appropriate in order to create a more inviting and welcoming image. On the other hand, a ratio of 1:1 may result in a flat and uninteresting image that lacks dimensionality. Ultimately, the light intensity ratio is an important factor in achieving the desired look and feel in three-point lighting.

Do I Need Three Lights in My Setup?

It is not necessary to use three lights in three-point lighting. While a traditional three-point lighting setup typically uses three lights - a key light, a fill light, and a backlight - there are a number of alternatives that can be used. For example, the key light can be substituted with the sun or a window, depending on the location of the shoot. Similarly, the fill light can be replaced with a reflector, bounce card, or other white surface that reflects the key light back at the subject. This can include materials like white card stock, poster board, or even a white wall. By using these substitutions, it is possible to create a three-point lighting setup with fewer lights than the traditional setup.

Remember that:

1.   Key light: The key light is the main light source in the 3 point lighting system. It is usually placed to one side of the subject and is used to provide the main source of illumination. The key light should be bright enough to provide adequate illumination, but not so bright that it creates harsh shadows or washes out the subject.

2.   Fill light: The fill light is used to soften the shadows created by the key light and to provide a more even illumination of the subject. It is usually placed on the opposite side of the key light and is set to a lower intensity.

3.   Back light: The back light is used to separate the subject from the background and to create a sense of depth in the shot. It is placed behind the subject and is pointed towards the back of the head or shoulders.

By using a 3 point lighting system, you can create professional-quality lighting for your video footage that is balanced, flattering, and engaging. Whether you are making a film, a television show, or a YouTube video, a 3 point lighting system is a valuable tool for creating visually striking, dynamic footage that engages and entertains your audience.

Lights For a 3-Point Lighting System

There are many different types of lights that can be used in a 3 point lighting system. The best lights for your specific needs will depend on the scale and complexity of your production, as well as your budget and other factors. My favorites are LEDs. LEDs will turn on instantly, produce far less heat, do not use much energy and often you can both dim and change their colors from your cool to warm whites. They are extremely versatile when filming.

The only drawback is they can be expensive initially if you want all the features, that being said they are reducing in price each year. Also, they are often non-replaceable (but last 10,000 hours usually) so just keep that in mind if you are on a budget.

Another thing to keep in mind is to make sure to get high-quality versions if you are also going the LED route as poor-quality LEDs definitely show on film. Below I have included the four main lights one would use for filming using our Three Point System.

1.   Incandescent lights: Incandescent lights are traditional light bulbs that use a filament to produce light. They are relatively cheap and widely available, but they can generate a lot of heat and are not very energy efficient.

2.   Fluorescent lights: Fluorescent lights are energy-efficient lights that use a gas-discharge process to produce light. They are relatively cool to the touch and are a good choice for large, continuous lighting setups.

3.   LED lights: LED lights are energy-efficient lights that use a semiconductor to produce light. They are extremely energy efficient and can be dimmed or colored to suit the needs of your shoot.

4.   Studio lights: Studio lights are powerful, professional-grade lights that are commonly used in film and television production. They are typically more expensive than other types of lights, but they offer a high level of control and can be used to

create a wide range of lighting effects.

Shadows

Where there is light, there is shadows. Shadows can have a big impact on the overall look and feel of a shot in a video. They can add depth, dimension, and visual interest to a shot, as well as create mood and atmosphere.

There are a few key ways that shadows can affect a shot:

1.   Depth: Shadows can add depth to a shot by creating the illusion of a third dimension. For example, if you are shooting a subject with a light source behind them, the shadows that are cast on the subject will create the impression of depth and separation between the subject and the background.

2.   Dimension: Shadows can also add dimension to a shot by

creating the impression of volume and mass. For example, if you are shooting an object with a light source to one side, the shadows that are cast on the object will create the impression of volume and mass.

3.   Mood: Shadows can also create mood and atmosphere in a shot. For example, using low-intensity lighting and long shadows can create a moody, atmospheric shot, while using high-intensity lighting and short shadows can create a more vibrant, energetic shot.

4.   Visual interest: Shadows can also add visual interest to a shot by creating patterns and textures. For example, if you are shooting through a window or through a patterned screen, the shadows that are cast on the subject can create interesting patterns and textures.

Lighting a "Let's Play" Video

Now we understand lighting and shadows and we are looking to film a "Let's Play" video which features a talking head or the gamer from waist up. I have listed some practical things to remember and a few tips for setting up the lighting for a "Let's Play" video showing the YouTuber playing computer games:

1.   Use a combination of natural and artificial light: A combination of natural and artificial light can help to create a well-balanced and visually appealing shot. Try setting up your computer and camera near a window to take advantage of natural light, and supplement it with artificial light sources as needed.

2.   Use soft lighting: Soft lighting can help to create a more

natural and inviting look in your shots. You can achieve this by using softbox lights or by diffusing the light with a softbox or another light modifier.

3.   Use a backlight: A backlight can help to separate the YouTuber from the background and add depth to the shot. You can achieve this by placing a light source behind the YouTuber, or by using a reflector to bounce light back onto their face from behind.

4.   Pay attention to shadow: As we just mentioned, shadow can add depth and dimension to your shots, but you don't want it to be too harsh or distracting. Pay attention to the direction and intensity of your light sources and adjust them as needed to create the right balance of shadow and highlight.

5.   Use color temperature to create mood: The color temperature of your light sources can affect the overall mood and atmosphere of your shots. Warm light sources, such as tungsten lights, can create a cozy, warm atmosphere, while cool light sources, such as fluorescent lights, can create a more clinical, neutral atmosphere. Experiment with different color temperatures to find what works best for your particular needs.

CHAPTER 6: AUDIO

While it's easy to focus on the visual elements of a video, such as lighting and composition, the audio is just as important in creating an engaging and professional-looking video.

Poor audio quality can ruin even the most visually stunning video. Imagine trying to watch a video with muffled or distorted sound – it's simply not enjoyable. On the other hand, clear and well-balanced audio can make all the difference in the viewing experience, enhancing the overall impact of your video.

It's not just the quality of the audio that matters, but also the content. Good audio helps to convey your message and keep your viewers engaged. Whether you're recording a voiceover, music, or sound effects, it's important to take the time to plan and execute good audio for your video.

So, if you're planning to create a YouTube video, don't neglect the audio! Invest in a good quality microphone and take the time to record in a quiet location. Your viewers will thank you.

I want to delve further into the technical aspects of good audio in video production. While it's important to have a clear and well-balanced audio track, there are a few other technical considerations to keep in mind as well.

One important factor to consider is the microphone. Using a good quality microphone can make a big difference in the sound of your video. There are many types of microphones available, each with their own unique characteristics and suited to different recording situations. For example, a shotgun microphone is great for recording dialogue and is often used on set, while a lavalier microphone is a small, unobtrusive option that is often used for interviews.

Another factor to consider is the recording environment. It's important to find a location that is as quiet as possible to avoid background noise. If you're recording in a noisy environment, such as a city street, you may want to use a microphone with a directional pickup pattern to help reduce background noise.

In addition to the recording environment, it is a good idea to use a digital audio workstation (DAW) to edit and mix your audio. A DAW allows you to adjust the levels of different audio tracks, apply effects such as EQ and compression, and balance the overall audio mix. There are many DAWs available, both free and paid, so it's worth taking the time to find one that works best for your needs.

Though Audio is important during the filming stage, I will go into this aspect of production in more depth in both our Complete Guide and Editing Guide in the series.

Microphone Quality

The quality of the microphone you use can have a big impact on the final audio of your video. Different microphones have different characteristics that make them more or less suitable for different recording situations. Below I have listed a few factors to consider when choosing a microphone:

1.   Polar pattern: The polar pattern of a microphone refers to the way it picks up sound. There are several different polar patterns, including cardioid, omnidirectional, and figure-eight. Cardioid microphones are highly directional and are best for recording a single sound source, such as a voice or instrument. Omnidirectional microphones pick up sound equally from all directions, making them good for recording groups or ambient sounds. Figure-eight microphones pick up sound from the front and back, but not from the sides.

2.   Frequency response: The frequency response of a microphone refers to the range of frequencies it can pick up. Some microphones have a wider frequency response than others, which can affect the overall clarity and detail of the sound.

3.   Sensitivity: The sensitivity of a microphone refers to how well it can pick up faint sounds. A more sensitive microphone will

be able to pick up quieter sounds, but may also be more prone to picking up background noise.

4.   Dynamic range: The dynamic range of a microphone refers to the difference between the loudest and quietest sounds it can handle. A microphone with a wide dynamic range can handle a greater range of volumes, which can be useful in situations where there are sudden changes in volume.

5.   Connectivity: Finally, consider the connectivity of the microphone. Some microphones use a wired connection, while others are wireless. Wireless microphones can be more convenient, but may also be prone to interference.

Overall, the best microphone for your video will depend on your specific needs and the recording situation. It's a good idea to try out a few different microphones and see how they affect the final audio of your video.

Is the iPhone Enough?

I often get asked if the audio from an iPhone is good enough for YouTube videos. The short answer is: it depends. While the audio from an iPhone can be of good quality, there are a few factors to consider when deciding if it's suitable for your particular video.

One important factor to consider is the type of iPhone you have. newer iPhones, such as the iPhone 12, have improved audio capabilities and can produce high-quality audio. However, older iPhones may have more limited audio capabilities and may produce lower-quality audio.

Another factor to consider is the type of audio you are recording. If you are recording voiceover or a single sound source, the iPhone's built-in microphone may be sufficient. However, if you are recording music or multiple sound sources, you may want to consider using an external microphone to capture higher-quality audio.

Just remember, you need to consider the overall quality of your video. If you are shooting in good lighting and using a stable camera setup, the audio from your iPhone may be sufficient. However, if you are shooting in low light or with a shaky camera, the audio may be more prone to distortion or noise.

Reducing Background Noise

Again, I can't stress enough the importance of a quiet recording environment when it comes to creating a successful video. Background noise, such as traffic, construction, or even the sound of your own breathing, can be a major distraction for your viewers and undermine the overall quality of your video.

So, how can you get your recording environment ready to reduce background noise? Here are a few tips:

1.   Choose the right location: Look for a location that is as quiet as possible. This might be a room in your home that is away from windows and other sources of noise, or a studio or recording booth. If you're shooting in a public location, try to find a spot that is isolated from noise.

2.   Use a directional microphone: A microphone with a directional pickup pattern, such as a shotgun or cardioid microphone, can help to reduce background noise by focusing on sound from a specific direction. This is especially useful if you're shooting in a noisy environment or want to record a single sound source.

3.   Use a noise gate: A noise gate is a tool that mutes audio below a certain volume threshold. This can be useful for eliminating low-level background noise, such as the sound of your own breathing or the hum of a computer.

4.   Use foam or other sound-absorbing materials: Placing foam or other sound-absorbing materials around the recording area can help to reduce echo and other types of noise. This is especially useful if you're shooting in a room with hard surfaces, such as tiles or concrete.

CHAPTER 7: FILMING LOCATION

Like most of the things we have discussed so far, location where you shoot your YouTube video can have a big impact on the final product.

Choosing a good film location is an important aspect of producing a video because it can significantly impact the final product. The right location can help set the tone and atmosphere of the video, as well as provide a visually appealing backdrop for the action. On the other hand, a poorly chosen location can distract from the content of the video and make it less effective. When selecting a film location, it is important to consider factors such as lighting, noise levels, and accessibility. It is also important to ensure that the location aligns with the theme and style of the video, and to obtain any necessary permits or permissions to film there. Ultimately, taking the time to carefully choose a good film location can help to enhance the overall quality and impact of a video.

In addition to these practical considerations, the film location can also play a role in the storytelling of the video. By choosing a location that is relevant or meaningful to the subject matter, the video can become more immersive and impactful. For example, if the video is about a historical event, filming at the actual location where the event took place can add a sense of authenticity and depth. Similarly, if the video is set in a specific time period, choosing a location that reflects the architecture and design of that era can help to transport the viewer back in time. Ultimately, the film location can be used to convey a sense of place and help to enhance the overall narrative of the video.

Here are a few tips for choosing the right location for different types of YouTube genres:

Travel Channels:

When filming for a travel channel, the location is especially important. Choose a location that is visually appealing and representative of the destination you are showcasing. Consider the lighting, architecture, and any local landmarks or cultural points of interest.

Food Review Channels:

If you're filming a food review, the location should be clean and well-lit. A cluttered or distracting background can be a major distraction for your viewers. Consider shooting in a restaurant or other food-related setting, or use a neutral backdrop such as a plain wall or table.

For Let's Play Channels:

If you're filming a Let's Play video, the location may not be as important as the gameplay itself. However, it's still a good idea to choose a location that is well-lit and free of distractions. A clean, clutter-free desk or tabletop can work well for this type of video.

Remember, the location of your video is just one factor to consider when creating a successful YouTube video. It's important to also consider the audio, lighting, and composition of your shots to create a professional and engaging video.

CHAPTER 8:
SHOOTING SCHEDULE

A shooting schedule is a detailed plan that outlines the specific shots, locations, and other elements that will be captured during the filming of a movie, television show, or other video production. It is typically created by the director and the director of photography (DP) and is used to coordinate the logistics of the shoot, including the cast and crew, the locations, the equipment, and the overall schedule.

A shooting schedule typically includes a breakdown of each day's filming, with a list of the specific scenes, shots, and locations that will be filmed. It may also include details about the cast and crew, such as the names of the actors and the roles of the crew members, as well as information about the equipment and resources that will be needed for each day of filming.

The purpose of a shooting schedule is to ensure that the filming process runs smoothly and efficiently, and to help the director and DP plan and coordinate the overall look and feel of the film. By following a shooting schedule, the director and DP can ensure that they are capturing all the necessary footage and can make any necessary adjustments to the schedule as needed.

Whether you are making a short film, a feature film, or a television show, a shooting schedule is an essential tool for organizing and coordinating the production process. By understanding the principles of shooting schedules and how to create one, you can create professional-quality films that engage and entertain your audience.

Should I Even Bother with A Shooting Schedule?

Whether or not you need a shooting schedule for your YouTube videos will depend on the scale and complexity of your production. If you are making a simple, one-shot video, such as a vlog or a how-to video, you may not need a detailed shooting schedule. However, if you are making a more complex video, such as a documentary or a narrative film, a shooting schedule can be a helpful tool for organizing and coordinating the production process.

A shooting schedule is not necessarily intended to make your YouTube videos more "professional," but rather to help you plan and coordinate the production process and ensure that you are capturing all the necessary footage. By following a shooting schedule, you can ensure that you are using your time and resources effectively and can make any necessary adjustments to the schedule as needed.

Overall, whether or not you need a shooting schedule for your YouTube videos will depend on the specific needs of your production. If you are making a simple video, a rough outline or shot list may be sufficient. However, if you are making a more complex video, a shooting schedule can be a valuable tool for organizing and coordinating the production process.

Single Day Shooting Schedule Example:

How-To-Video

Customarily with these guides, I like to give both practical and specific steps/examples which help put the theory into practice.

Say you were making a woodworking, how-to video. Below I have listed an example of a shooting schedule for your video that shows how to make a desk within a single day, incorporating technical terms such as white balance, shot composition, and lighting:

9:00am:

- Set up shop and gather materials
- Measure and mark out the dimensions of the desk
- Cut the pieces for the desk legs

11:00am:

- Assemble the desk legs
- Cut the pieces for the desk top

1:00pm:

- Assemble the desk top
- Sand and finish the desk

3:00pm:

- Set up lighting and adjust white balance for intro and overview shots
- Film intro and overview of the project, paying attention to shot composition and lighting
- Film close-up shots of each step of the process, adjusting white balance as needed
- Film final reveal of the completed desk, focusing on shot composition and lighting

5:00pm:

- Edit and publish the video, paying attention to color grading and other post-production elements

When filming and scheduling these How-to videos, it is important to remember shot composition and lighting for the audience to appreciate the work and understand what they need to do themselves. Proper shot composition can help highlight the details of the project and make it easier for the viewer to follow along. This includes using close-up shots to show intricate details and wide shots to give context to the project as a whole. Lighting is also crucial in a How-to woodworking video, as it can help to showcase the texture and color of the materials being used. Poor lighting can make it difficult for the viewer to see what is happening and understand the instructions being given. By paying attention to shot composition and lighting, you can create a more engaging and informative video for your audience.

Filming a Travel Blog

Film Schedule

Day 1:

- Arrival in Split and check-in to accommodation

- Orientation tour of the city and scouting out locations for future shots

- Lunch at a local restaurant and filming food and atmosphere

- Visit to Diocletian's Palace and filming exterior shots and history segments

- Dinner at a seafood restaurant and filming food and

atmosphere

Day 2:

•   Early morning shots of the city, including the Riva waterfront and Marjan Hill

•   Breakfast at a local bakery and filming food and atmosphere

•   Visit to the Split City Museum and filming segments on the history of the city

•   Lunch at a traditional Croatian restaurant and filming food and atmosphere

•   Afternoon visit to the Bacvice Beach and filming segments on local recreation and relaxation

•   Dinner at a rooftop restaurant with views of the city and filming food and atmosphere

Day 3:

•   Early morning visit to the Split Market and filming segments on local produce and food culture

•   Breakfast at a local café and filming food and atmosphere

•   Visit to the Mestrovic Gallery and filming segments on the artwork and history of the museum

•   Lunch at a local taverna and filming food and atmosphere

•   Afternoon visit to the Klis Fortress and filming segments on the history and views from the fortress

•   Dinner at a Mediterranean restaurant and filming food and atmosphere

Day 4:

•   Early morning visit to the Split Archaeological Museum and filming segments on the history and artifacts of the city

•   Breakfast at a local café and filming food and atmosphere

•   Visit to the Galerija Meštrović and filming segments on the history and artwork of the museum

•   Lunch at a local restaurant and filming food and atmosphere

•   Afternoon visit to the Marjan Park and filming segments on the nature and recreation in the park

•   Dinner at a traditional Croatian restaurant and filming food and atmosphere

Day 5:

•   Early morning visit to the Split Art Gallery and filming segments on the history and artwork of the gallery

•   Breakfast at a local café and filming food and atmosphere

•   Visit to the Split Ethnographic Museum and filming segments on the history and culture of the city

•   Lunch at a local restaurant and filming food and atmosphere

•   Afternoon visit to the Marjan Hill and filming segments on the nature and views from the hill

•   Farewell dinner at a seafood restaurant and filming food and atmosphere

- Departure from Split

Remember, it does not need to be super in-depth or technical. You just need to know the basics. Your first few videos will always have things you would love to improve (even your 50th video if I'm being honest). But by remembering to add little reminders to your shooting schedule you can take full advantage of your potential for success with each video.

Different Videos Require Different Plans

If we are looking at our two examples specifically, our shooting schedules and plans are different for how-to videos and travel vlogs because they have different purposes and goals. How-to videos typically focus on teaching the viewer a specific skill or technique, and as a result, they often require a more structured and planned approach to filming. This might involve setting up specific shots or angles in advance, rehearsing the steps being demonstrated, or using props and other visual aids to help illustrate the point being made.

On the other hand, travel vlogs are often more spontaneous and unscripted, as they are meant to capture the feeling of being in a new place and experiencing it in the moment. As such, shooting schedules for travel vlogs may be more flexible and open-ended, allowing for more flexibility and room for improvisation. The focus is often on capturing the atmosphere and culture of a destination, rather than following a specific script or set of instructions.

CONCLUSION

By following the tips and techniques outlined in this book, you can improve the quality of your YouTube videos and better engage with your audience. With a little practice and experimentation, you will find your own unique style and be well on your way to creating successful and memorable videos for your channel.

Remember, the name of the game is branding. You want your brand to be special, unique and hopefully by reading my guides, high quality.

Note From the Author

Dear Readers,

As always I want to sincerely thank you for taking the time to read my books in my series. I hope that the information provided in these pages has been helpful and that you are now better equipped to create engaging and professional content for your channel.

If you have any questions or comments about the book, please don't hesitate to reach out to me. I am always happy to help and support aspiring YouTubers in any way I can.

Again, thank you for your support and I hope that you have found my book to be a valuable resource.

Ben

www.ingramcontent.com/pod-product-compliance
Lightning Source LLC
Chambersburg PA
CBHW071551260726
48653CB00007BA/2758